PRAISE FOR *THE*

"I have rarely come across such an encouraging, practical, and informative book all rolled into one! Robin Cox combines Scripture, church history, the quotations of the saints over the centuries, and prayer with a wealth of practical advice, exhortation, and examples of simple 'tasks' as we draw alongside of' others in the mold of Barnabas. A book to read in one sitting and also one to dip into daily."

—ALASTAIR REID, GENERAL SECRETARY, THE INDEPENDENT SCHOOLS' CHRISTIAN ALLIANCE

"Have you ever wondered how powerful encouragement is? Robin Cox has. So much so, he has given his life to encouraging others to pursue God's purpose. Now he helps us do the same, by exploring the life and motivation of Barnabas. He provides multiple practical examples of how we can emulate this great leader, from opening a door to adopting a child. Buy the book, read the book, then release the book's message in others."

—GRAHAM COYLE, CHAIRMAN, EUROPEAN EDUCATORS' CHRISTIAN ASSOCIATION

"If you knew you could change the world for Jesus what would you do first? As I read Robin's latest book I was humbled by his simple but profound words of encouragement. We are called to love God with all our heart, soul, and mind, and love our neighbor as ourselves, but how? *The Barnabas Prayer*, in all its simplicity, shows us what it truly means to not just be believers, but followers of Christ."

—PAUL BROWNING, HEADMASTER, ST. PAUL'S SCHOOL

"Robin Cox skillfully takes us on a journey towards being an encourager, using a prayer as the map. At each location he provides insightful quotes, reflection questions, relevant historical data, and practical 'to do' lists, all of which motivate us to continue the journey. At our destination we find ourselves knowing more about Barnabas and the early church. We also have a practical framework within which to explore the possibilities of serving others through encouragement."

—MARION SANDERS, HEAD OF THE SCHOOL OF TEACHER EDUCATION, BETHLEHEM TERTIARY INSTITUTE, NEW ZEALAND

"*The Barnabas Prayer* by Robin Cox is a timely, richly layered, inspirational book that speaks to the needs of people all over the world in these tumultuous times. Deeply appalled by the dastardly things humans can do to other humans, Cox seeks not to blame or accuse, but instead asks what God wants him to *do*. I warmly recommend this text in which Cox gently takes us by the hand and invites us to share in this journey of love in action, giving multiple practical suggestions to inspire you and me to show love in action in our own communities."

—RUDI PAKENDORF, LUTHERAN LAY LEADER IN SOUTH AFRICA AND THE UNITED STATES

"An inspiring book filled with plenty of highly practical real-life examples, *The Barnabas Prayer* is a thought-provoking read. We need a generation of people willing to follow in the footsteps of Barnabas and this book is a good place to start reflecting on what that journey might look like."

—HILARY HAGUE, NATIONAL DIRECTOR, SCRIPTURE UNION NZ

The Barnabas Prayer

To Nicky and Pippa
with sincere appreciation
and gratitude — for Alpha
and your ministry.
God Bless,
Robin Cox

Numbers 6:24-26

Also by Robin Cox

The Mentoring Spirit of the Teacher—Inspiration, support and guidance for aspiring and practising teacher-mentors

Expanding the Spirit of Mentoring—Simple steps and fun activities for a flourishing peer mentor or peer support program

Nurturing the Spirit of Mentoring—50 fun activities for young people and for peer mentor training

Encouraging the Spirit of Mentoring—50 fun activities for the ongoing training of teacher-mentors, volunteer mentors, student leaders, peer mentors and youth workers

The Spirit of Mentoring—A manual for adult volunteers

Letter 2 a Teen—Becoming the Best I can Be

Making a Difference—The Teacher-Mentor, the Kids and the M.A.D Project

7 Key Qualities of Effective Teachers: Encouragement for Christian Educators

Mentoring Minutes: Weekly Messages to Encourage Anyone Working with Youth

The Spirit of Mentoring Series (eBooks):

Book 1: More tips, strategies and 167 Fun ideas for the mentoring journey

Book 2: More tips, strategies and true stories to develop meaningful mentoring relationships

Book 3: More tips, strategies and 234 Discussion topics for the mentoring journey

More information available at www.yess.co.nz

The Barnabas Prayer

Becoming an Encourager in Your Community

Robin Cox

RESOURCE *Publications* · Eugene, Oregon

THE BARNABAS PRAYER
Becoming an Encourager in Your Community

Resource Publications
An Imprint of Wipf and Stock Publishers
199 W. 8th Ave., Suite 3
Eugene, OR 97401

www.wipfandstock.com

PAPERBACK ISBN: 978-1-7252-8961-1
HARDCOVER ISBN: 978-1-7252-8962-8
EBOOK ISBN: 978-1-7252-8963-5

01/29/21

In memory of the thousands
of young children who passed
through Terezin Concentration Camp (1942–44)
and whose artwork and poetry
deeply impacted my heart and soul—
always remembered.

Fall is here.
The leaves turn yellow on the trees,
The campfire dies out.
My thoughts are far from here,
Somewhere far,
Where integrity lives.

It lives in my friend.
Now I think of her.
Memories gather 'round me
Like the falling leaves.
—ANNA LINDTOVA[1]

1. Extract from the poem, *Campfire (to Eva Landova)*, written by Anna Lindtova at Terezin Concentration Camp. Anna Lindtova was born on March 19, 1930. She was deported to Terezin from Prague on May 12, 1942. She died at Auschwitz on October 28, 1944. Volavkova, *I Never Saw Another Butterfly*, 67.

Contents

Areas where Barnabas helped set up the early church

Awakening—the Call

Let God do his work in you, and concentrate on living a
selfless life in each and every moment, as though each
moment was the whole of eternity.

—FENELON

*Reflection: How do you know when God calls you?
How do you respond? What feelings do you experience?*

In 2016, shortly before my retirement, my wife and I undertook
a "River Cruise," travelling from Budapest in Hungary, and ultimately completing this memorable experience in Prague, Czech
Republic.

As a History teacher, I had always wanted to travel beyond
the "Iron Curtain" and to visit parts of Eastern Europe.

Three life-changing visits

Three specific sightseeing visits are permanently fixed in my mind,
as each brought out the brutality of Nazi and Communist oppression and tyranny and moved me deeply.

The first visit was "Shoes on the Danube Promenade," Budapest's holocaust memorial situated on the Pest side of the river
(east bank) between two famous landmarks, the Chain Bridge and
the Parliament Building.

This haunting and chilling memorial comprises sixty pairs of life size, iron shoes cast in the style of the 1940s, representing the 600,000 Hungarian Jews who died during World War Two. This memorial was created sixty years after the war by film director Can Togay and the sculptor Gyula Pauer.

The memorial is dedicated to the approximately 20,000 Jews who were executed along the river bank between 1944 and 1945 by members of the Hungarian fascist and antisemitic organization the Arrow Cross Party. The victims were forced to remove their shoes and face the executioner. They were shot so they fell into the river, their bodies carried away, allegedly to save the Arrow Cross Party from having to dig graves. Shoes were a valuable commodity at the time and could be sold by the executioners.

The second visit was to the "House of Terror" museum located at 60 Andrassy Boulevard, Budapest. The museum contains exhibits related to the fascist and communist regimes in twentieth century Hungary. It is also a memorial to the victims of these regimes, including those detained, interrogated, tortured, or killed in the building.

The building was initially the headquarters of the Arrow Cross Party. Later it became the headquarters for the State Security Authority (the AVH) run by the Soviet Union which suppressed any rebellions and opposition to its brutal rule.

Thousands of people were executed by the Arrow Cross Party and the AVH, many of them in this building.

The third visit was to the Terezin Concentration Camp—the ghetto of Terezin (Theresienstadt)—located in the hills outside Prague, which was created by the Nazis to cover up the Jewish genocide. 15,000 children under the age of fifteen passed through Terezin Concentration Camp between 1942 and 1944. Fewer than one hundred children survived.

We visited the Jewish Quarter in the Old Town Prague and saw the tributes to all who died in the Holocaust, which included some of the children's artwork. At Terezin we saw more of the artwork and I was deeply moved—the parent and teacher in me brought to tears by mankind's inhumanity.

How many times had I heard the challenging instructions of Jesus?

> Love the Lord your God with all your heart and with all your soul and with all your mind (Matt 22:37).
> and
> Love your neighbor as yourself (Matt 22:39).

How could I respond? What could I do with the time I have left on this planet to help create a better, more compassionate, and caring global community?

Prayer and reflection

I resorted to more prayer and reflection as I sought God's direction. I felt overwhelmed by everything I had experienced on this trip.

I had lived in southern Africa for much of my life before moving to New Zealand with my family in 1999. From a young age I had a deep concern for disadvantaged people, which was linked to a slowly evolving Christian faith. I witnessed the heresy of apartheid and the oppression and suffering of millions of disadvantaged people. During the 1980s and early 1990s I organized youth symposia in South Africa bringing together young people and teachers of all races and cultures to break down these barriers and prepare for a post-apartheid South Africa.

> Approximately 6,000 students and teachers attended these symposia. Participants listened to influential speakers, discussed ways to work together to prepare for a post-apartheid South Africa, debated, dramatized controversial topics, played sport, laughed and cried together. Lives were enriched—my own included—and changed forever as barriers between races broke down.[1]

Later I developed conflict resolution and life skills workshops for youth of all races and cultures, undertook a variety of projects

---

1. Cox, *7 Key Qualities*, 9.

to support disadvantaged children, and my wife and I began sponsoring children in different parts of Africa and in India.

In 2012 I facilitated some education workshops in India where I was confronted by poverty wherever I travelled. The school I was working at in Australia had also launched a wonderful outreach program to Vanuatu and I had the privilege of visiting the schools with which we interacted. Yet again I was confronted by poverty on a scale I struggled to comprehend.

In August 2016, having returned from our travels, I was in a space where I stood tall in God's grace that embraces my brokenness, and wrote two prayers. The Global Prayer for Peace was framed by the Declaration of Human Rights. I pray this prayer every week, as a reminder that God is working out his plan for the world and I have a responsibility to play my small part in obedience to his will.

Global Prayer for Peace

Father God,

embrace all nations with a vision of global peace.

Transform the hearts and minds of all people that they might capture this vision of peaceful co-existence and collaborative living,

and let it begin with me.

Encourage me not to rest until I know that our global community is free and as equal as is humanly possible.

Help me to speak out with courage and boldness against discrimination and injustice.

Guide our global leaders to rid their countries of any unjust and oppressive laws, guaranteeing their people freedom of thought, religion, speech and movement.

Protect us from the evils of tyranny and the abuse of fundamental Human Rights and give me the strength to speak out against such atrocities.

Raise up global leaders committed to ending war, global poverty and injustice.

Create a global village in which all peoples have the right to affordable housing, medicine, education, childcare and have sufficient to live.

Use me to reach out to those less privileged without expecting anything in return.

Help me to understand my duty to my fellow men, women and children and to play my small part in ensuring their freedom and rights are protected.

Gently nudge me each and every day to remember that the change begins with me.

Let me never cease striving to play my small part in establishing a global community built on freedom, justice and peace.

In the precious name of Jesus, I pray.

Amen.

The second untitled prayer I have prayed every day since I wrote it:

Jesus, let me see with your eyes,
hear with your ears,
reach out with your hands,
walk your talk with your feet,
and love with your love.

God clearly spoke into my heart and encouraged me to explore ways to love my neighbor as myself and to give greater meaning in my life to his instruction to "Love the Lord your God with all your heart and with all your soul and with all your mind" (Matt 22:37).

Enter Barnabas

I have been fortunate to work through two cancer scares, the first when I was a young boy and was dangerously ill, and the second, a few years ago. These experiences help me to empathize with those who suffer, to champion the underdog, and to guide or mentor many adolescents, one of my life passions linked to my other passion, teaching.

God has blessed me with the gift of encouragement. A former teaching colleague thanked me for the help I had offered through a challenging time with these words: "You are an incredible *blessing and encourager! A true Barnabas (Acts 4:36)."* I still feel humbled when I read these words.

Many students and teaching colleagues I mentored, coached, or taught have expressed their thanks for the encouragement I offered them, which inspired me to write *Mentoring Minutes: Weekly Messages to Encourage Anyone Working with Youth.* The book includes stories of my mentors, as well as those I have mentored over the years, and hundreds of tips and strategies to encourage anyone working with youth.

I am inspired by the *many* people who serve God with unrelenting courage and perseverance. However, I still feel helpless and overwhelmed when I observe the suffering of those in refugee camps, the ongoing racist attacks in different parts of the world, people suffering under oppressive dictatorships, and most especially those stark images of suffering children that I am confronted with on a daily basis.

I feel that I can do more.

In 2020 the global community experienced a pandemic with the outbreak of COVID-19, a disease caused by a coronavirus which (at the time of writing) has killed over one million people.

As COVID-19 spread across the world causing unprecedented lockdowns in most countries, I felt God nudge me to write this book about a Biblical character who has fascinated me for many years, the apostle Barnabas. Perhaps this process would help me explore ways I could make a positive difference in my community and encourage others at the same time?

Why Barnabas?

We are introduced to Barnabas for the first time by Luke in Acts 4:36–37, after the Holy Spirit came at Pentecost (Acts:2):

> Joseph, a Levite from Cyprus, whom the apostles called
> Barnabas (which means "son of encouragement"), sold a
> field he owned and brought the money and put it at the
> apostles' feet.

From the outset, Barnabas—who is mentioned twenty-nine times in the New Testament—displays a selflessness which God uses to bring glory and praise to his name during the early years of the Christian church. Barnabas becomes a prophet, an apostle, a teacher, a miracle worker, and one of the most Christlike mentors the world has seen.

Barnabas was born in Cyprus, the third largest island in the Mediterranean. Anthony and Cleopatra died after the naval Battle of Actium in September 31 BC and Cyprus came under the direct control of Augustus (also known as Octavian) the first emperor of Ancient Rome. In 22 BC Augustus made Cyprus a senatorial province governed by a proconsul.

Cyprus had profitable agricultural lands, forestry—many Roman ships were built from Cyprus timber—and silver mining. Cypriots worshipped the Greek gods and goddesses Aphrodite, Zeus, Isis, and Apollo.

The first Christian churches are established during times of economic stress. Barnabas responds to this crisis. He reveals his strength of faith, character, and total commitment to Jesus with his financial gift from the sale of his land which he places at the feet of the apostles with no stipulations.

Barnabas was a Levite—descendants of Levi, the third son of Jacob and Leah and a member of the tribe of Levi (Deut 10:8)—a priestly class which performed minor supportive duties and tasks in the temple. So, he held a certain status in the Jewish community at the time. As he places the money at the feet of the apostles, this humble gesture suggests that he sees rank in the kingdom as different from his status in society.

Barnabas appears to be earmarked as a positive person of influence, described by author and professor of theology Robin Branch[2] as "a 'people person', a natural minister and effective leader."

2. Branch, *Barnabas*, 300.

I often wonder how Barnabas felt when he made the commitment to follow Jesus, especially when I think about his strong Jewish roots and the possible impact of his decision on his family relationships.

The Barnabas Prayer

I continued to reflect on the untitled prayer I had written after returning from my Eastern Europe trip and saw how this prayer seemed to describe Barnabas in so many ways. Yet something was missing. I was working on my book to encourage teachers: *7 Key Qualities of Effective Teachers: Encouragement for Christian Educators,* so I was thinking and researching around the topic of servant leadership transforming communities. More prayer took place.

I also continued my research about this remarkable apostle, his humility, fallibility, courage, genuine goodness, unswerving faith, big-heartedness, and his selfless example of servant leadership.

One day—over three years after I returned from Eastern Europe—the extra words flowed from my pen: "connect with your heart." The finishing touches could be added to The Barnabas Prayer.

The Barnabas Prayer

Jesus, let me see with your eyes,
Hear with your ears,
Reach out with your hands,
Walk your talk with your feet,
Connect with your heart,
And love with your love.
In your precious name, I pray.
Amen.

Becoming a rippler—walk in the footsteps of Jesus

Mother Teresa's well-known words have motivated and encouraged me to step out of my comfort zone more times than I can remember:

> I alone cannot change the world, but I can cast a stone
> across the waters to create many ripples

Love your neighbor. . .

Everyone can become a "rippler"—one who, empowered by the Holy Spirit, selflessly creates ripples as they spread God's unconditional love and grace in their family, community and beyond, as modeled by Jesus, then Barnabas.

We are born in the image of God. He has given us unique gifts and talents to bless others.

> So Christ himself gave the apostles, the prophets, the evangelists, the pastors and teachers, to equip his people for works of service, so that the body of Christ may be built up until we all reach unity in the faith and in the knowledge of the Son of God and become mature, attaining to the whole measure of the fullness of Christ (Eph 4:11–13).

> Now you are the body of Christ, and each one is a part of it. And God has placed in the church first of all apostles, second prophets, third teachers, then miracles, then gifts of healing, of helping, guidance, and of different kinds of tongues (1 Cor 12:27–28).

Let us unpack The Barnabas Prayer and explore key moments in his life. We will explore dozens of ways—because we each have unique gifts and talents—we can individually and collaboratively contribute when we become ripplers who transform our communities through our selfless acts of service, as we follow in the footsteps of Barnabas and respond to God's call on our lives. I am still learning about my gifts and talents and find myself trying out some of these ideas, often with surprisingly positive feelings.

We can appreciate how important it is to spend more time *telling people that God believes in them* and less time urging people to believe in God.

As my faith increases, I feel encouraged and emboldened to become more and more involved in my community. My life priorities are changing in many positive ways, as I feel Jesus conversing with me: "Are you a believer in Christ, or a Christ follower? What actions tell me and others you are a Christ follower?"

Love the Lord your God. . .

> Blessed are the poor in spirit,
> for theirs is the kingdom of heaven (Matt 5:3).

The Beatitudes, or Blessings, which introduce Jesus' Sermon on the Mount, teach me that "true happiness comes from looking at life from God's perspective, which is often the reverse of the human point of view."[3] I am becoming a more authentic Christian disciple, modeled so effectively by Barnabas, with a deeper understanding of how to become an encourager in my community.

This is the first Beatitude which encourages me to remain humble, with a deep appreciation of Jesus' teaching that *all* my blessings originate from God's unconditional love and grace. God enables me to undertake his will for my life as I experience an openness, an inner peace and a total dependence on him alone. I admit my fragile nature, repent and ask God to reveal areas I can work in to praise and glorify him. As I grow in faith, I find it easier to reach out to others and walk in the footsteps of Jesus.

The Beatitudes are woven through the pages of this book to encourage us to respond boldly, as Barnabas did, to our call to become *selfless followers* of Jesus. They encourage us to step out of

---

3. *Word in Life Bible*, 1418.

our comfort zone, use the gifts and talents we are blessed with and continually strive to be Christlike in our relationships with others.

I thought you might find this story about my journey interesting and valuable, perhaps an encouragement if you also often feel overwhelmed by the local and global challenges which confront us every day. Please join me on this journey as we explore Barnabas' life and consider the different opportunities for us to make positive ripples in our communities.

As we make our choices, we honor those children who spent time in the Terezin Concentration Camp, as well as the millions of others who have had their lives taken from them at too young an age.

Influential missionary and founder of the China Inland Mission (now the Overseas Mission Fund International) James Hudson Taylor[4] might have had Barnabas in mind when he wrote these words of encouragement and hope for all who become involved in kingdom work:

> Let us see that we keep God before our eyes, that we walk in his ways and seek to please and glorify him in everything, great and small. Depend upon it, God's work, done in God's way, will never lack God's supplies.

4. Taylor, *Hudson Taylor's Spiritual Secret*, 121.

Jesus, let me see with your eyes

I am doing what I will do for all eternity. I am blessing God,
praising him, adoring him, and loving him with all my
heart.
—Brother Lawrence

*Reflection: Reflect on the way you view the world around you
most of the time—your family, your relationships, and your
local or wider community? Which part of your community
would you like to see transformed? How do you discern what is
and is not of Jesus?*

The Barnabas' approach

Tradition—not recorded in the Bible—suggests that Barnabas was
taught by Gamaliel, one of the leading first century AD Jewish
scholars. Barnabas immersed himself in study, and was encouraged by God's Word so he could effectively encourage others and
become a teacher of sound doctrine.

Barnabas became a follower of Jesus, accompanied him during his Galilean ministry, and was thought to be one of the seventy-two sent out by Jesus in pairs to preach and heal on his behalf to

> . . . every town and place where he was about to go. He told
> them, "The harvest is plentiful, but the workers are few.

Ask the Lord of the harvest, therefore, to send out workers
into his harvest field. Go! I am sending you out like lambs
among wolves. Do not take a purse, or bag or sandals, and
do not greet anyone on the road" (Luke 10:1–4).

There were further instructions (Luke 10:5–16) and Barnabas
probably learnt from the experience how important it is to focus
on the personal growth and development of kingdom workers
while undertaking kingdom work. The result? "The seventy-two
returned with joy and said, 'Lord, even the demons submit to us in
your name'" (Luke 10:17).

Luke only uses the name Joseph ("may God increase") once
in Acts (Acts 4:36)—the Hebrew name is Joses ("he that pardons").
Thereafter he uses the name Barnabas, "son of encouragement."

In the New Testament *paraklesis* is the word most often
translated "encouragement." It comes from the Greek word *para*—
"alongside of"—and *kaleo*—"to call." Therefore, we can understand
how Barnabas, the "encourager," was regarded by the disciples and
fellow apostles as someone who was called to come alongside another person to guide, or help renew and comfort them.

Parakletos is the Greek word for Holy Spirit. The similarity
between *paraklesis* and *parakletos* is clear. When Barnabas [or any
Christian] surrenders to the Holy Spirit, he becomes a source of
encouragement to others. Businessman and pastor Bill Palmer[1]
wrote:

> In essence, Barnabas was known not just for offering a
> few words of encouragement or comfort, but for stand-
> ing beside people in their trials. He was not emotion-
> ally detached from them, but joined with them in their
> troubles.

Jerusalem was the key city of Judea, the center of its economic, political, and religious life. Jewish leaders continued to
plot ways to stamp out the remnants of Jesus' movement after his

---

1. Palmer, *Learning from Barnabas*.

recent crucifixion. Yet, despite the dangers and the hostile environment, Jesus had instructed his disciples to begin their ministry in Jerusalem.

Should the disciples succeed and spread the gospel throughout Jerusalem, the good news would in all likelihood be carried throughout the whole of Judea—the home of *pure* Judaism—and eventually into Samaria. Samaria had been colonized with non-Jews by the Assyrians in the seventh century BC. Many non-Jews intermarried with the Israelites and this had created bitter tension between Samaria and Judea.

Barnabas becomes a significant agent of change during these early days of the church. He changes the course of history when he befriends Saul, the persecutor of Jews—also a student of Gamaliel—who had witnessed the stoning to death of Stephen (Acts 7:58) before he was converted on the road to Damascus (Acts 9:1–19). Saul was on his way to Damascus to round up followers of Jesus and "take them as prisoners to Jerusalem" (Acts 9:2).

> When he [Saul] came to Jerusalem, he tried to join the disciples, but they were all afraid of him, not believing that he really was a disciple. But Barnabas took him and brought him to the apostles. He told them how Saul on his journey had seen the Lord and that the Lord had spoken to him, and how in Damascus he had preached fearlessly in the name of Jesus (Acts 9:26–27).

Barnabas' gift of encouragement is evident as he appears to see God's grace in the most unlikely people—the murderer Saul, and later among the uncircumcised gentiles in Antioch. Barnabas is clearly sensitive to the leading of the Holy Spirit as he welcomes Saul as a fellow apostle. He listens to Saul, sees his potential through the eyes of Jesus and believes him. Robin Branch[2] writes:

> Every instance in Acts presents Barnabas as one who wholeheartedly follows the Lord Jesus, is available for kingdom purposes, and readily gives himself to God's service.

2. Branch, *Barnabas*, 317.

Barnabas unselfishly vouches to the disciples for Saul's integrity as a genuine disciple of Jesus. He displays empathy, a spirit of forgiveness, courage, and wisdom at a time when most of Jesus' disciples are understandably suspicious of Saul and his motives—an exemplary lesson in the cost of discipleship.

The manner in which Barnabas welcomes Paul, mediates between him and the other disciples, and continues to coach and mentor him for a while, reminds us that, when we look at situations through the eyes of Jesus as best as we can, his Spirit will empower and direct us how best to serve him. Our apparently small contribution can change our community—the world—for the better.

The influential nineteenth century preacher Phillip Brooks[3] said:

> Go and try and save a soul and you will see how well it is worth saving, how capable it is of the most complete salvation. Not by pondering upon it, nor by talking of it, but by serving it you learn its preciousness.

Learning from Barnabas—look through the eyes of Jesus

Our Christian walk has many challenges. We are encouraged because we know that God equips us with the resources, and gives us the strength to cope with these challenges when we need it and not before. We imagine ourselves walking in the footsteps of Barnabas as we reflect on areas of our life we can develop with the help of the Holy Spirit. Author and educator Graham Coyle[4], shares some words of encouragement: "I am convinced when we are operating with sensitivity to the Holy Spirit, we can leave results up to Him."

- We become an authentic follower of Jesus—our role model—and learn how life is *always* about giving God the praise and glory. We put our ego aside, look to Jesus for direction, and

3. Wiersbe, *50 People*, 155.
4. Coyle, *To Infinity*.

gain a deeper understanding of the meaning and practice of unconditional love.

- We focus on others when we communicate with them and listen carefully to what they share. We care about their happiness, welfare, and spiritual growth.

- We learn how to look behind the mask through the eyes of Jesus and see the beauty of others within and outside. We look for opportunities to *selflessly* affirm, encourage, and guide. We become pro-active and speak to the potential in others.

- We genuinely express a spirit of forgiveness in our relationships with others. Influential early twentieth century evangelist Evan Roberts[5] said: "It is no use asking God to forgive you, unless you have forgiven your enemies. You will only be forgiven in the same measure as you forgive."

- We *always* look for God's bigger plans—signs of God at work—and prayerfully see how we can encourage others to see his plans fulfilled.

Becoming a rippler—in the footsteps of Barnabas

We often feel overwhelmed by personal, community, and global issues. What can we do? Where do we start? This is too hard . . . God presents us with many opportunities to use our unique gifts and talents to bless and encourage others. We learn how to look at life through the lens of Jesus, and remain available for the Holy Spirit to prompt us. Here are a few ideas which may help us become active followers of Jesus.

Love your neighbor. . .

- See a need and respond. Be creative: make cards, help with gardening, building, computers, events; send a birthday card

5. Stead and Campbell Morgan, *The Welsh Revival*.

or a note of encouragement to someone who feels lonely; send someone an e-card for a special occasion.

- Leave cash to pay for someone after you in a shop.
- Help someone repair a flat tire or a car that has broken down.
- Let someone ahead of you—with a friendly smile and wave— if you are driving and stuck in a queue.
- Welcome strangers or people who look lost or out of place.
- With an authentic smile, hold the door open for someone.
- Leave a tip with a "thank you" note.
- Offer to drive someone to church, or the doctor, or the shops, or to an appointment.
- Give up your seat—with an authentic smile—for someone on public transport or in a waiting room.
- Willingly pick up something dropped by someone.
- Look for creative ways to authentically celebrate the achievements of others.

Love the Lord your God. . .

Blessed are they who mourn,
for they will be comforted (Matt 5:4).

We regret our sinful nature and express a desire to renew and improve ourselves, and to follow God's way in righteousness. We acknowledge that we cannot handle the challenges of life in our own strength. We pray for the fruit of the Holy Spirit, and find ourselves wanting to do more—to stretch ourselves—to praise and glorify God as we seek Jesus' face in our interactions with others. "But the fruit of the Spirit is love, joy, peace, forbearance [patience], kindness, goodness, faithfulness, gentleness and self-control" (Gal 5:22–23).

- Offer a surprise gift to someone—a free movie or dinner voucher, for example, or make an anonymous donation (in kind, or money) when you hear of a need.

- Offer to do hair, makeup and nails for the high school students for their formal or prom, or for an elderly person.

- Organize—or offer to assist with—a collection of new unused makeup and perfume to donate to disadvantaged people, or a shelter for victims of abuse, or for the homeless.

- Volunteer to help with a neighborhood or community group that paints over graffiti.

- Donate a Christmas tree to a nursing home and, with the help of some friends, decorate it.

- Give a homeless person a meal, or prepare a meal for a homeless shelter.

- Organize a community Easter egg hunt in your neighborhood to bring joy to some children.

- Plant a tree in your neighborhood, or as part of a community project. Volunteer to help in a local environmental project—for example, the clean-up of a local waterway, beach, river, lake, or ponds.

- Volunteer to be trained as a lifeguard at your local beach or pool.

- Set up a neighborhood facility to voluntarily repair neighbors' appliances.

- Offer a lift to a hitch-hiker—be prayerfully discerning.

> God is able to take the mess of our past and turn it into a message. He takes the trials and tests and turns them into a testimony.
> —Christine Caine

Hear with your ears

Do not have your concert first, and then tune your instrument afterwards. Begin the day with the Word of God and prayer, and get first of all into harmony with him.

—JAMES HUDSON TAYLOR

Reflection: Think of a time when you felt especially close to God. What happened? How do you discern God's voice or his gentle nudge?

The Barnabas' approach

In Acts—which immediately follows John's gospel in the New Testament—Luke continues to write about what happens after Jesus returns to heaven and his followers begin to share the gospel in other parts of the Roman Empire.

Syrian Antioch was the center of the early Christian movement, the third largest city of the Roman Empire and ultimately the headquarters of New Testament Christianity. Situated on the Orontes River in Cappadocia, Antioch was well known for its corrupt and luxurious lifestyle enjoyed by many of its people. Reverend William Thomas Stead and Reverend Doctor George Campbell Morgan[1], writing about life in Wales in 1905, echo these

1. Stead and Campbell Morgan, *The Welsh Revival*.

early Christian days and leave us wondering why we struggle so often to learn from history:

> Always there is the winter of corruption, of luxury, of indolence, of vice, during which the nation seems to have forgotten God, and to have given itself up to drunkenness, gambling, avarice and impurity. Men's hearts fail them for fear, and the love of many grows cold.

The Council of Jerusalem hears how the apostles, who had scattered after the killing of Stephen, were successfully sharing the "good news about the Lord Jesus" (Acts 11:20–21) among the Greeks in Antioch. They decide to send Barnabas, clearly regarded as a trusted and discerning apostle, to check out what was actually happening in Antioch (Acts 11:22).

Barnabas' visit to Antioch appears to mark the beginning of his missionary work as an influential spiritual leader. We see his gift of encouragement in action as he explores what is happening there.

> When he [Barnabas] arrived and saw what the grace of God had done, he was glad and encouraged them all to remain true to the Lord with all their hearts (Acts: 11:23).

Barnabas does not appear to be judgmental or critical of the Gentile believers. Rather, he discerns God's grace at work and is pleased with what he sees and hears. He encourages these faithful believers to continue their good work living by God's grace and mirroring that grace in their relationships with others.

We glimpse Barnabas' maturity, wisdom, and discernment as a spiritual leader who inspires and empowers others to use their God-given gifts and talents to point people to Jesus.

Why was this possible? "He was a good man, full of the Holy Spirit and faith" (Acts 11:24).

Barnabas is available to do kingdom work to honor and glorify God wherever he is sent. He models the importance of being in tune with the Holy Spirit as evangelist David du Plessis[2] reminds

2. Liardon, *The Smith Wigglesworth Prophecy*, 171.

us: "only the Holy Spirit is the water of life that will quench the thirst of the human soul."

Barnabas appears to envision what God is doing in Antioch. He focuses on a positive message of hope as he offers encouragement to his fellow believers. Hope allows Jesus' followers to take prayerful and calculated risks as they trust God to bless their efforts—". . . and a great number of people were brought to the Lord" (Acts 11:24).

Learning from Barnabas—listen with the empathy of Jesus

We have the opportunity to share our faith sensitively, yet assertively and with humility, when we develop meaningful relationships with other people. We can reflect on some possible areas to continually cultivate during our Christian journey.

- We focus fully on the person speaking to us; mirror body language; watch tone of voice and eye contact. We respect cultural differences (when appropriate), other viewpoints, and the uniqueness of others.

- We listen prayerfully to what is being said *and* to what is not being said; we listen for feelings; we hear and feel—empathize—the pain, anxiety, fear, happiness, courage, and passion others share with us.

- We allow the speaker to finish their sentence before we respond. We briefly summarize what we hear to make sure we understand what the speaker shares.

- We keep an open mind, remain teachable at all times, and are available to listen to diverse viewpoints.

- Prayerfully—guided by the Holy Spirit—we strive to be a faithful peacemaker or mediator in challenging situations. We learn to think before we speak, especially in conflict situations. We look at conflict situations with a positive attitude and remember that sometimes it is better to focus on the facts alone and to put emotions aside.

- We listen to praise and worship music, link with Christian media and podcasts, or read Christian books and resources. We do whatever we can to stay tuned in to the Holy Spirit's guidance.

Becoming a rippler—in the footsteps of Barnabas

There are many ways we can respond to the call to support and encourage others if we learn how to sharpen our ears to the cries of those around us. God only asks us to do something he knows we can do with his help, and with our God-given gifts—"I can do all this through him who gives me strength" (Phil 4:13). Here are a few ideas for consideration.

Love your neighbor. . .

- Respond to a call for help in your church—a welcomer, car park assistant, cleaner, kitchen helper, musician, mentor, drama or dance coach, prayer warrior, church library assistant, or a coworker in some other church activity.

- Compliment and thank people who work on the frontline— for example, your local checkout operator, librarian, roadworks workers, police, or garbage collector.

- If, for example, you have been hospitalized, send a thank you note to a special doctor or nurse who has spent significant time conversing with you.

- Model good sportsmanship—be a humble winner and a graceful loser.

- Donate some coins to a student busking in your community.

- Authentically promote the ideas and efforts of others—for example, comment on a blog, or share information about a friend's initiative about which you have heard.

- Respond to the call to support recycling projects.

- When you hear and observe a stressful situation such as a parent or family relative struggling with a child at the local store or playground, say something kind, positive, and encouraging.

- Respond to a call to create homemade gifts for others—jams or baked items, baby clothing, knitted scarves, jerseys, or blankets.

- Respond to a request to facilitate—or help facilitate—a collection of blankets or other items for a garage sale, for example, to donate proceeds to a needy cause.

- Voluntarily respond to a call to facilitate—or help facilitate—the collection of used glasses (eye glasses), including sun glasses, for donation to an organization that collects, cleans, repairs and distributes them to people in need.

Love the Lord your God. . .

Blessed are the meek,
for they will inherit the earth (Matt 5:5).

Our humility encourages us to become gentle and kind even in the face of adversity. We acknowledge how much we need God's help in our daily lives. We do our best to follow the example of Jesus, display self-control, and submit to the will of our faithful God. He encourages us to hear the cries of those in distress and reach out to them with a compassionate and non-judgmental heart as we seek to bring peace to a broken world. We begin to take small, tentative steps to become more involved in our community. We appreciate the guidance of the Holy Spirit and God's assurance that we are never alone. "Have I not commanded you? Be strong and courageous. Do not be afraid; do not be discouraged, for the Lord your God will be with you wherever you go" (Josh 1:9).

- Collect "freebies" for donations to others, and personally deliver them when you hear of a need.
- Donate art supplies or other requested resources to children in a homeless shelter.
- Respond and assist with a church charity project or a foodbank.
- Host a church visitor.
- Offer to help repair or paint a homeless shelter or be part of a team to maintain a homeless shelter's garden.
- Host or facilitate a small group—fellowship, Bible study, and prayer.
- Respond to a call to become a children's ministry teacher.
- Respond to a call to teach an adult to read or speak a foreign language.
- Respond to a call to read to kids at a local school, or, where appropriate, volunteer to walk kids home from school.
- Respond to the call to reach out to youth, for example, as a sport coach, music teacher, or babysitter.
- Volunteer as a crisis counselor at a teen center, or for Lifeline.

Jesus first, others next, and yourself last spells J-O-Y.
  —Linda Byler

Reach out with your hands

Is prayer your steering wheel or your spare tire?
—CORRIE TEN BOOM

Reflection: What are your strengths? How are these strengths helping you to live out your calling? How do you feel about reaching out to others when you are required to move out of your comfort zone?

The Barnabas' approach

Almost *every* appearance of Barnabas in the New Testament finds him encouraging others in their faith walk at some point. "He serves as the supreme model for how to mentor young believers,"[1] and models Jesus' important commandment: "Love your neighbor as yourself" (Matt 22:39).

Barnabas has spent time with Saul. He has observed Saul's potential and believes in him. No doubt their many conversations about their respective faith walks contribute to Barnabas' discernment that God will use Saul in a mighty way.

Barnabas is unlike many of his fellow Jewish believers, as he chooses not to ignore the Gentile believers, but rejoices at how God has reached out to them and uses them so powerfully in Antioch.

1. *Word in Life Bible*, 1681.

Barnabas believes that Saul, a converted Jewish follower in recent years, could be just the person to teach the new converts in the expanding Antioch church, and to reconcile any possible misunderstandings between the churches in Antioch and Jerusalem. After all, Saul has a captivating story to share with non-believers, as well as a story to encourage believers.

In about 43 AD Barnabas reaches out to the forgotten Saul, with humility and discernment, a number of years after the latter's conversion, and so begins one of the most transformative ministries in the history of the Christian church.

> Then Barnabas went to Tarsus to look for Saul, and when he found him, he brought him to Antioch. So, for a whole year Barnabas and Saul met with the church and taught great numbers of people. The disciples were called Christians first in Antioch (Acts 11:25–26).

Saul—soon to become Paul—fashions and shapes the church as we know it today, and writes at least seven—possibly thirteen— New Testament books. However, Barnabas emerges as one of *the* most influential figures who establishes these early churches to which approximately 2.3 billion people are linked today.

Barnabas models the challenges involved in following the selfless, sacrificial example of Jesus. He knows there is a cost when he invites Saul, the former persecutor of Jews, to Antioch. Barnabas models forgiveness, encourages Saul to share his story, and also inspires new believers to forgive Saul for his previous actions.

God is the God of the extraordinary. He takes two Jewish converts—"outsiders" in a way, one from Cyprus, the other from Tarsus—to lead the outreach to *foreign* communities of Gentiles and Jews and to spread the gospel.

Unlike most of the other disciples (Acts 4:13), Barnabas and Saul are well educated. They reconstitute the "message" and make it applicable to these new believers, and as an encouragement to the Jews in those communities to embrace a "new way." After only one year, Barnabas and Saul gain the trust of these new converts through their authentic witness. Initially these new believers were called followers of "the Way" (Acts 9:2). Now the first disciples of Jesus in Antioch are called "Christians."

Barnabas and Saul also model how a developing Christlike life requires faithfulness to the gospel message and lifestyle. Retaliation and rebellion against the Roman rulers are not the Jesus' way. They build a movement of Christians which crosses gender, ethnic, language, geographic, and economic boundaries in places like Antioch and Jerusalem. The birth of a multilingual international church occurs.

Barnabas and Saul invite visiting prophets like Agabus to share with the church (Acts 11:27). Agabus stands up "and through the Spirit predicted that a severe famine will spread over the entire Roman world. (This happened under Claudius)" (Acts 11:28). New converts immediately gather gifts "to provide help for the brothers and sisters living in Judea. These gifts were then sent to the elders by Barnabas and Saul" (Acts 11:29–30).

As we reflect on the emergence of the early church, author and teacher Christine Fletcher[2] reminds us of the importance of building positive relationships in a faith community.

> The key to their success seemed to lie in the Greek word *koinonia*, which is translated as fellowship in Acts 2:42. . . . what lies at the heart of this word is "sharing." This comes across clearly in their sharing of possessions and money and their sharing of meals, including the breaking of bread. . . . Real relationships that went beyond superficial friendships seem to have been a major factor in demonstrating the reality, love and transformational power of Christianity. Such meaningful sharing is needed more than ever today, when so many people are longing for closer relationships and lack a sense of belonging.

Learning from Barnabas—reach out with the hands of Jesus

At no point does the life of Barnabas suggest that he is perfect—far from it, as is seen further into his ministry. However, he clearly

2. Fletcher, *Encounter with God*, 80.

continues to develop the Christian values which he probably witnessed Jesus model. We can reflect on ways we can strive to develop a Christlike approach to life as we reach out to others, and continually remind ourselves that we never walk this road alone—Christ before us, Christ beside us, Christ behind us.

- We volunteer our time and possessions generously and prayerfully—guided by the Holy Spirit. We are responsible, reliable, and honest guardians and stewards of God's possessions as we reach out to those in need, and expect nothing in return.

- We remain faithful, trustworthy, and display a positive growth mindset as we reach out and share messages of hope with others.

- When we reach out to others, this often might come at a personal cost. We remember that we are *never* alone after we surrender our life in totality to Jesus.

- We remain humble as we learn how to place the needs of others before our own.

- We reach out with empathy and identify the strengths of others. We name these strengths and, where possible, encourage them how to use these strengths to further the kingdom work.

Becoming a rippler—in the footsteps of Barnabas

When we reach out to others, we take the attention away from ourselves and focus on the health and wellbeing of others. Barnabas appeared to do this wherever he went. We learn how to leave our fingerprints in positive ways in our community. The following are a few ideas for consideration.

Love your neighbor. . .

- Prayerfully present your tithes or financial offerings—or offerings in kind—for the growth of the Christian church community.

- Offer to return a shopping cart when emptied by an elderly or incapacitated person in the car park.

- Grow your hair long and donate your ponytail—for example—to an organization that makes wigs out of real hair for cancer patients.

- Donate clothing, furniture, household goods, toys, books, sports equipment, or puzzles to those in need—declutter your home or place of work.

- Invite someone for a meal, or share leftovers from a meal with someone in need.

- Buy someone a tea or coffee, a lunch or dinner, or some other refreshment.

- Surprise someone with a birthday cake.

- Put together care packages (clothes, toiletries, education supplies) for the homeless and disadvantaged.

- Make bags, or purses, or jewelry out of recycled materials as an example to others of how to raise environmental awareness.

- Offer to shop for someone who is homebound for any number of reasons.

- Nominate someone for a special award within your place of work, the community, or the country, or praise someone at work for a job well done.

Love the Lord your God. . .

> Blessed are those who hunger and
> thirst for righteousness,
> for they will be filled (Matt 5:6).

We develop a stronger desire for justice and righteousness. We have a renewed hunger to obey and depend on God as we seek this righteousness. God equips us with the resources and skills to reach out to the fallen and broken with actions and messages of hope. He gives us the courage to step faithfully out of our comfort zone: "Trust in the Lord with all your heart and lean not on your own understanding; in all your ways submit to him and he will make your paths straight" (Prov 3:5–6).

- Organize a car wash with a group of friends and donate all proceeds to charity.

- Volunteer to proofread eBooks for Project Gutenberg, for example—a library of over 60,000 free eBooks.

- Shovel snow from a neighbor's walk or path (where relevant); offer to take your neighbor's garbage bin to the street curb and return it; mow your neighbor's lawn, or wash their car, or bring firewood into their home.

- Sponsor a child and financially support missions, or become involved in some supportive way with missionary work.

- Gather some friends and put on a drama or music performance for the elderly, or for children in hospitals.

- Volunteer to sponsor an animal at the local zoo, or volunteer to help at an animal shelter.

- Volunteer to build birdhouses or bird feeding trays in your neighborhood to raise environmental awareness.

- Help a young couple learn how to budget.

- Volunteer to become involved in a social justice issue that is close to your heart—prayerfully seek God's guidance.

- Volunteer to tutor a student who struggles with academic studies, or offer free music lessons, especially to the disadvantaged.

- Become a foster parent.

  Overcomers are not perfect. They fail just like the rest of us, but they keep on getting up, keep on repenting, and keep on being willing to surrender themselves to Christ and letting him, who is the only perfect one, work through them.

  —Nancy Missler

Walk your talk with your feet

I think I am willing to bear whatever God sees fit to lay
upon me. Let my dear heavenly Father inflect the keenest
anguish, I will submit, for he is infinitely excellent and can
do nothing wrong.

—HARRIET NEWELL[1]

*Reflection: Think about a time you went the extra mile to
reach out to someone. What happened? How do you feel about
that experience? When do you find it easiest to reach out to
others and expect nothing in return?*

The Barnabas' approach

Luke introduces us to Barnabas again in Acts after he and Saul
deliver the gifts for Judea from the Antioch believers to the church
in Jerusalem.

> When Barnabas and Saul had finished their mission,
> they returned from Jerusalem [to Syrian Antioch], tak-
> ing with them John, also called Mark (Acts 12:25).

John Mark was Mary's son (Acts 12:12) and Barnabas' neph-
ew (Col 4:10), a young man Barnabas will encourage and mentor,

1. Adams, *Harriet Newell*, 86.

no doubt because the Holy Spirit guides him to see John Mark's potential as a Christian witness.

Back in Antioch, Barnabas models servant leadership. His obedience to God's call on his life is clear, as is his willingness to go wherever God wishes to send him. Yet, critical to this are the power of prayer and listening for the movement of the Holy Spirit to lead and confirm these calls on his heart.

> Now in the church at Antioch there were prophets and teachers. Barnabas, Simeon called Niger, Lucius of Cyrene, Manaen (who had been brought up with Herod the tetrarch) and Saul. While they were worshiping the Lord and fasting, the Holy Spirit said, "set apart for me Barnabas and Saul for the work to which I have called them." So, after they had fasted and prayed, they placed their hands on them and sent them off (Acts 13:1–3).

About 46 AD the church commissions Barnabas, Saul, and John Mark—the first Christian missionaries to be sent overseas[2]—to set off on a missionary trip around Asia Minor cities in the eastern Mediterranean region of the Roman Empire.

Barnabas models how to follow Jesus and use one's strengths in response to God's call on one's life. He recognizes Paul's clear gifts in oratory and leadership, for example. Barnabas reveals his humility as he steps back from the leadership role with which he has been entrusted, to allow Paul, as he became known (Acts 13:9), to step up.

Barnabas does not appear to seek the limelight, nor does he appear to shrink back from God's call on his life. "He models how we can live out our calling and gifts in a complimentary way to others who serve the larger cause—a wonderful example of servant leadership."[3]

Barnabas and Paul travel to Seleucia, south of Antioch in Syria, and sail to Cyprus, arriving at Salamis, the principal city at the time, where an influential Jewish community lives. "They proclaimed the word of God in the Jewish synagogues . . . traveled

2. Taylor, *The Bible Journey*.
3. Rudi Pakendorf, email correspondence with Robin Cox, 3 June 2020.

through the whole island until they came to Paphos" (Acts 13:5–
6), where the proconsul Sergius Paulus witnesses Paul blinding his
assistant, the sorcerer or false prophet Elymas [Bar-Jesus]. Elymas
tries to sway the proconsul from the Christian faith. "When the
proconsul saw what had happened, he believed, for he was amazed
at the teaching about the Lord" (Acts 13:6–12).

> From Paphos, Paul and his companions sailed to Perga in
> Pamphylia, where John Mark left them and returned to
> Jerusalem. From Perga they went on to Pisidian Antioch
> (Acts 13:13–14).

Pisidian Antioch, named after Antiochus, King of Syria after
the death of Alexander the Great, has a large Jewish population, is
an important trading center, and also home to many retired members of the Roman army—potential Gentile converts.

Here Paul enters the synagogue on the Sabbath and shares
an outline history of the Jewish people with all in attendance, including the "God-fearing Gentiles." He also shares about Jesus' life,
death, resurrection, and the message of salvation (Acts 13:13–41).

Barnabas and Paul are invited to speak again at the next Sabbath where "almost the whole city gathered to hear the word of the
Lord. When the Jews saw the crowds, they were filled with jeal-
ousy. They began to contradict what Paul was saying and heaped
abuse on him" (Acts 13:44–45).

Paul and Barnabas face persecution from the Jews. The early
church movement arrives at the crossroad as Paul lays down the
challenge to all in attendance:

> We had to speak the word of God to you first. Since you
> reject it and do not consider yourselves worthy of eter-
> nal life, we now turn to the Gentiles. For this is what the
> Lord has commanded us:
> 'I have made you a light for the
>   Gentiles,
> that you may bring salvation to the
>   ends of the earth' (Acts 13:46–47).

God has used Barnabas to mentor and train Paul for this significant ministry. The unassuming and selfless Barnabas, whose courage in the face of opposition from the Jews, and whose loyalty to Paul is unquestionable, is God's key agent of change as the early church is established. He continues to model integrity and faithfulness—"now faith is confidence in what we hope for and assurance about what we do not see" (Heb 11:1). The result? "The word of the Lord spread through the whole region" (Acts 13:49).

> Our aim should not be greatness, but humility. We must learn to love personal obscurity and contempt, so that our only concern is to glorify God.
> —Fenelon[4]

The actions of Barnabas and Paul remind us how obedience to the Holy Spirit transforms individual lives and communities. This is wonderfully expressed in a verse from the hymn or song *Here is Love* written by William Rees[5] in 1900 and based on John 3:16 and 1 John 4:10:

On the Mount of Crucifixion
Fountains opened deep and wide;
Through the floodgates of God's mercy
Flowed a vast and gracious tide;
Grace and love like mighty rivers
Poured incessant from above
And heaven's peace and perfect justice
Kissed a guilty world in love.

Barnabas and Paul again face persecution from the Jewish leaders and are expelled from the region. Undaunted, they travel to Iconium, ready for the next challenge. "And the disciples were filled with joy and with the Holy Spirit" (Acts 13:52). Iconium is a "wealthy town at the heart of a prosperous agricultural area in Southern Galatia . . . and an important Roman military base."[6]

4. Fenelon, *Let Go*, 14.
5. Penn-Lewis, *The Awakening in Wales*.
6. Taylor, *The Bible Journey*.

Learning from Barnabas—walk with the feet of Jesus

The decision to follow Jesus is a personal choice which we can *never* force on another person. So often it is our kindness, a non-judgmental attitude, or an expression of unconditional love—in other words, our *actions*—that draw people to want more information about the Christian faith. Educator Graham Coyle[7] writes:

> Jesus was good at pacing himself. He was never in a hurry. He frequently told people he was only giving his time and attention to the things his Father was doing (John 5:19; 8:28). That's why he always appeared to be in control and never panicked. If he didn't sense it from heaven, then he didn't allow it into his life. His agenda and timetable were determined by his relationship with the Father.

- We model the values of Jesus wherever we go with courage and a joy-filled heart.

- Teamwork, loyalty, and a collaborative spirit are powerful witnesses of Jesus in action in our life.

- We give of ourselves and our possessions until it hurts, for this is a Christlike attitude; serving Jesus often comes at a great personal cost. James Hudson-Taylor[8] describes the reality of the Christian walk, epitomized by the example of Barnabas:

> There is a needs-be for us to give ourselves for the life of the world. An easy, non-self-denying life will never be one of power. Fruit-bearing involves cross-bearing. There are not two Christs—an easy-going one for easy-going Christians and a suffering, toiling one for exceptional believers. There is only one Christ. Are you willing to abide in *Him*, and thus to bear much fruit?

7. Coyle, *To Infinity*.
8. Taylor, *Hudson Taylor's Spiritual Secret*, 240.

- Status and rank mean nothing when we follow in the footsteps of Jesus and undertake kingdom work—a steadfast trust and focus on Jesus is the key.

- Selfless leadership sometimes involves stepping back graciously and—with humility—allowing others to lead. We are respected and remain a positive person of influence.

- We are willing to walk in obedience to God's call on our heart—and this sometimes involves walking some extra miles. We pray and fast as we discern his will for us, and how we can most effectively serve him. Charles Finney[9] wrote these encouraging, though challenging words:

> At every step you tread on chords that will vibrate to all eternity. Every time you move, you touch keys whose sound will re-echo all over the hills and dales of heaven and through all the dark caverns and vaults of hell.

Becoming a rippler—in the footsteps of Barnabas

There are a variety of opportunities to reach out to others and "walk the talk" in the footsteps of Jesus. We leave our footprints for others to follow. Here are more ideas for consideration as we aim to use our God-given gifts and talents to make a positive difference in our community.

Love your neighbor. . .

- Help an older person cross the road or let them go ahead of you in a queue.

- Pick up clothes on the floor at the store, or items which have fallen off a shelf and replace them.

- Collect litter when you walk in your neighborhood, or on a country or mountain path, or on the beach.

9. Finney, *Lectures on Revivals*.

- Keep your emails positive—watch the tone of the wording. Build people up because that is what an encourager does.

- Give away produce from your garden.

- Bake cookies, or bread, or a meal to give to first-time visitors at your church, or place on a table at work.

- Reach out to someone in need with a gift certificate.

- Create an environment friendly garden—place a bird feeder and water fountain in the garden.

- Stop and greet a neighbor or someone else living in your neighborhood—just say hello and let the conversation flow.

- Offer to walk a disabled or elderly neighbor's pet.

- Offer to babysit a friend's child.

Love the Lord your God. . .

> Blessed are the merciful,
> for they will be shown mercy (Matt 5:7).

We acknowledge how much we need God's grace and mercy in our lives. We look, through the compassionate eyes of Jesus, at those who suffer, and appreciate at a deeper level the power of forgiveness, or a cry for help. This awakening allows us to reach out with God's unconditional love, embraced by the power of the Holy Spirit, to a friend, family member, or neighbor. We feel empowered to walk a little more boldly in the footsteps of Jesus, possibly inspired by one of these ideas. "For I know the plans I have for you," declares the Lord, "plans to prosper you and not to harm you, plans to give you hope and a future" (Jer 29:11).

- Volunteer in your community: give blood; assist at a food bank or soup kitchen; assist at an animal welfare organization or a bird sanctuary; or run errands for senior citizens.

- Buy someone a book or a puzzle they will enjoy as a surprise gift to show you care, or leave a devotional book or tract on a table at a restaurant or café.

- Help someone by offering to do their laundry or bringing a group of friends to clean their house or garden.

- Volunteer to help during an election.

- Organize a car pool or a school lift club to reduce car emissions and raise environmental awareness.

- Help a friend with a Do-It-Yourself (DIY) project.

- Organize a Christmas carol singing group and visit nursing homes or aged care facilities, or homes in your local neighborhood; offer to entertain or play music at a nursing home or aged-care facility; host a Bingo or games event.

- Write a letter to a community newspaper or contact a local radio station about an issue that is concerning you—focus on constructive engagement and, where possible, offer a positive solution or suggestion.

- Offer to speak at a career day.

- Offer to host an international student attending a school in your local community.

- Volunteer to run a pen pal program for kids—be a friend!

> Wherever the Lord sets you down, be all there! This is the message of Elijah and Elisha. You are the only "Bible" some people will ever read. Make sure you're a good translation.
> —Jim Elliott

Connect with your heart

*Reflection: How connected to God do you feel **most** of the
time? How can you discern this? What further little steps—
in this lifelong journey—can you take to strengthen this
connection?*

The Barnabas' approach

In about 47 AD, Barnabas and Paul continue to experience mixed
reactions from the Jews and Greeks to whom they speak in Iconium. They face more opposition from some Jews who "stirred up
the other Gentiles and poisoned their minds against the brothers"
(Acts 14:2). However, as long as they feel led by the Holy Spirit
they refuse to quit. They reveal the divine hearts that allow them
to teach and preach a spiritual, rather than an intellectual gospel.

> So, Paul and Barnabas spent considerable time there,
> speaking boldly for the Lord, who confirmed the mes-
> sage of his grace by enabling them to perform signs and
> wonders (Acts 14:3).

How do Barnabas and Paul grow in grace? Charles Finney, a leader in the Great Awakening in the United States during the nineteenth century, offers a possible reason as he shares some thoughts on how to grow in grace:

> You cannot have it too thoroughly impressed upon you that every step in the Christian life is to be taken under the influence of the Holy Spirit. The thing to be attained is the universal teaching and guidance of the Holy Spirit, so that in all things you should be led by the Spirit of God (Gal 5:16; Rom 8:6; Rom 8:13).

Eventually life becomes too dangerous (Acts 14:4–5), so Barnabas and Paul "fled to the Lycaonian cities of Lystra and Derbe and to the surrounding country where they continued to preach the gospel" (Acts 14:6).

Lycaonia was the capital of the Roman province in Central Asia Minor where there was a predominantly Greek population—more possible Gentile converts.

In Lystra Paul heals a man who has been lame from birth (Acts 14:8–10) and the crowd responds.

> When the crowd saw what Paul had done, they shouted in the Lycaonian language, "The gods have come down to us in human form!" Barnabas, they called Zeus, and Paul they called Hermes because he was the chief speaker (Acts 14:11–12).

Barnabas is called Zeus, the Greek god regarded as the supreme ruler of Mount Olympus. Zeus is depicted as an imposing and muscular man, so one assumes that Barnabas had both a spiritual and physical presence wherever he went.

Barnabas and Paul immediately respond with courage and humility to the crowd wishing to offer sacrifices to them.

> But when the apostles Barnabas and Paul heard of this, they tore their clothes and rushed out into the crowd shouting, "Friends, why are you doing this? We too are only human, like you. We are bringing you good news, telling you to turn from these worthless things to the

living God, who made their heavens and the earth and the sea and everything in them. . . ." Even with these words, they had difficulty keeping the crowd from sacrificing to them (Acts 14:14–15,18).

The Jews from Antioch and Iconium attack Barnabas and Paul. They stone Paul, but he is dragged from the city and rescued. Barnabas and Paul make their way to Derbe (Acts 14:19–20), where they continue to preach "the gospel in that city and won a large number of disciples" (Acts 14:21).

This whole period exemplifies the challenges facing the early Christian disciples. There are personal attacks, the relentless idol worship, and they face division among the people to whom they speak.

Yet Barnabas and Paul appear to be energized by the call on their hearts. As God's ambassadors, they undertake his work with joy and courage. It never appears to be a burden. They share a continuous message to these early Christians which they model—remain steadfast in the faith journey.

They plant new churches and leave behind a leadership system of newly appointed elders they can trust and continually encourage. "Prayer and fasting" (Acts 14:23) appear to be key aspects of their ministry on this missionary journey, together with obedience to the prompting and leading of the Holy Spirit—"Dear friends, do not believe every spirit, but test the spirits to see whether they are from God, because many false prophets have gone out into the world" (1 John 4:1).

As a result of the number of churches that are planted, the early Christian movement—pioneered by apostles like Barnabas—becomes the dominant philosophy and social force in the Roman Empire: " But you will receive power when the Holy Spirit comes on you; and you will be my witnesses in Jerusalem, and in all Judea and Samaria, and to the ends of the earth" (Acts 1:8).

Paul, the missionary, relying upon prayer and the dynamic power of the gospel, changed the face of the Roman Empire.[1]

Rather than quit on areas where they face hostile opposition, Barnabas and Paul display boldness and perseverance as they "returned to Lystra, Iconium and Antioch." Why? To strengthen and encourage the disciples there (Acts 14:22). They know that they are never alone and that God has gone ahead of them to prepare the way. Charles Finney[2] said: "You need to have a strong beating of your heart with his [God], or you need not expect to be greatly useful."

Fenelon[3], the seventeenth century Archbishop of Cambria, wrote of the challenges of Christian life, clearly evident as we follow Barnabas and Paul during these early church days:

> The Kingdom of God began at Calvary. The Cross was a necessity. When we pick up the cross of Jesus and bear it in love to him, his kingdom has begun in us. We must be satisfied to carry that cross as long as it is his will.

Barnabas and Paul remain positive Christian role models as they travel through Asia Minor on this first missionary journey. "We must go through many hardships to enter the kingdom of God" (Acts 14:22).

They travel from Pisidian Antioch through Pisidia—modern Turkey today—to Pamphylia, preaching in Perga—the regional capital in southern Central Asia Minor—then in Attalia, a key seaport on the coast of Pamphylia, before finally returning to Antioch in Syria.

> From Attalia they sailed back to Antioch, where they had been committed to the grace of God for the work they had now completed. On arriving there, they gathered the church together and reported all that God had done through them and how he had opened a door of faith to

1. Penn-Lewis, *The Awakening in Wales*.
2. Finney, *Lectures on Revivals*.
3. Fenelon, *Let Go*, 5.

the Gentiles. And they stayed there a long time with the disciples (Acts 14:26–28).

Learning from Barnabas—connect with the heart of Jesus

Our "heartfelt" attitude to the people with whom we interact can create life-changing moments for people who are lonely, lost or searching for some purpose and meaning in life. We reflect on the people who have positively impacted our Christian walk as we strive to be more like Jesus each day.

- We prayerfully learn how to express unconditional Christ-like love, care and help to those with whom we interact, as a compassionate and empathetic heart draws people to Jesus.

- We display a forgiving and non-judgmental heart as we connect with others. Evangelist David du Plessis[4] shares these insights:

  > . . . I had to learn to "walk in the way of love, just as Christ loved us and gave himself up for us as a fragrant offering and sacrifice to God" (Ephesians 5:2). That is why I like the verse: "This is how we know what love is: Jesus Christ laid down his life for us" (1John 3:16). That kind of love is unconditional. When I began to see this, things began to happen that I'd never seen before. . . . I could see that Jesus on the cross had granted unconditional forgiveness to the Jews who shouted, "Crucify Him!" and to the Romans, Jews, and Gentiles—that means all humanity. He had forgiven once and for all, and that was sealed with his blood.

- We celebrate the small spiritual victories in the power of the Holy Spirit as we connect with and support others.

- We are authentic, self-aware, yet assertive, and show respect and tolerance to those with whom we interact.

---

4. Liardon, *The Smith Wigglesworth Prophecy*, 187–188.

- Serving Jesus often comes at a personal cost when we set out to connect with others. We remain steadfast and keep our eyes upon Jesus. We persevere because God blesses those who honor him in their kingdom work.

- We seek to unify, not divide Christians. One of the reasons Christianity spread during Barnabas' lifetime was because the majority of Christians, irrespective of the church they belonged to, regarded themselves as members of a *common, connected Christian family.*

Becoming a rippler—in the footsteps of Barnabas

When we have a heart to serve Jesus, no matter the cost, the Holy Spirit moves us out of our comfort zone and uses us to reach out and connect with others. We learn how to develop the heartbeat of Jesus. The words that we share take on more importance (Appendix 1). Here are a few ideas to consider on how to be an effective witness to Jesus when we use our God-given gifts and talents to bless others and expect nothing in return.

Love your neighbor. . .

- Offer simple acts of service with a joyful heart: smile, hug, pray, make a friendly phone call, or send a message of encouragement.

- Take a welcoming meal to a new neighbor, a young couple with a baby, someone recuperating after an accident, someone who is grieving the loss of a loved one, or to someone who is struggling in any way.

- Write a blog or an article about a helpful topic and freely share it with others.

- Offer someone you have wronged an authentic apology— model Christian forgiveness.

- Introduce a friend to someone they don't know who might have similar hobbies, interests or careers.

- Turn off your cell (mobile) phone when connecting with and talking to others, or put it away.

- Promote happiness and joy—messages of hope—and combine this with a great sense of humor when you connect with others.

- Deliver a cake or cookies as a token of thanks to your local fire station, or police, or school, or library.

- Share your magazines or newspaper with others once you have read them.

- Organize a sponsored walk or ride for a charity of your choice—ask a friend to join you—and invite people to sponsor you.

- Foster a pet for a short time while it awaits a new home.

Love the Lord your God. . .

> Blessed are the pure in heart,
> for they will see God (Matt 5:8).

When we are pure in heart, we choose to be free of selfish purposes or intentions and self-seeking desires—our pride dissipates. In that space, Jesus assures us that we *will* see God. Surely this is something to strive for. Inspired by the example of Jesus' sacrificial love, we begin to give of ourselves to others in a spirit of selflessness empowered by the Holy Spirit. We contribute to the development of a happier, more peaceful local and global community—the ripple effect of our small actions. We dare ourselves to be more courageous, as we appreciate that God travels with us when we reach out to others: "Be strong and courageous. Do not be terrified because of them, for the Lord God goes with you; he will never leave you or forsake you" (Deut 31:6).

- Offer to house sit for a friend when they are away and look after their pets (even feed the goldfish!).

- Share stories or use social media platforms in *positive* ways to encourage and connect with others.

- Look for ways to *freely* share your creativity with others. Share your hobbies and gifts by teaching or coaching others how to garden, sew, bake, cook, play a musical instrument, maintain cars, repair computers, or use a new computer program.

- Volunteer to teach an elderly person a card game or trick; sit and read, or visit an elderly person—provide companionship.

- If you own a company or small business encourage your colleagues (or employees) to voluntarily serve others and lead the way. Allow them time off work to serve as a mentor, for example, in a school-based mentoring program.

- Adopt a pet, or offer to train a guide dog for the blind.

- Join a neighborhood watch group.

- Volunteer as a tour guide at your local art gallery or museum, or at some other community event.

- If you own a small business or company, provide work experience opportunities to youth exploring career options; offer an apprenticeship to a young person and personally mentor them through the experience.

- Volunteer to move alongside a refugee family to make them feel welcome in the community.

- Take a group of children or other people on a special trip—to the zoo, a circus, movie, museum, or to the local playground.

> Relying on God has to start all over every day, as if nothing has yet been done.
> —C. S. Lewis

and love with your love

...Amy Carmichael's emphasis for the rest of her life—to
reach out to the downcast and rejected, to love them, win
them to Christ, and build them up to help others.

—WARREN W. WIERSBE

*Reflection: In what ways do you feel Jesus expresses his love to
you? How do you receive it? Can you think of any time recently
when you passed this love on to others? What happened?*

The Barnabas' approach

Throughout his ministry Barnabas appears motivated to follow
Jesus no matter the cost. Prayer, fasting, fellowship with other
Christians, and the study and discussion of scriptures equips him
for his vital kingdom work. He is familiar with the way God used
people like Noah, Abraham, Moses, Isaac, Rahab, David, and Ruth
to undertake his kingdom work.

Barnabas continues to positively share the purpose and focus
of his life wherever he travels: ". . . he encouraged them all to remain true to the Lord with all their hearts" (Acts 11:23).

Now back in Syrian Antioch and a senior leader of the grow-
ing early Christian movement, Barnabas is caught up in a significant moment of church history.

The basic issue being propagated by a group of more traditional Jewish believers is that if the Gentiles are to be "saved" they must be circumcised (Acts 15:1). This will mean that the Gentiles have to embrace Jewish culture and Mosaic Laws—or Jewish rites—and turn away from their ethnic backgrounds. Such a move threatens to undo all the work Barnabas and Paul have undertaken with the Gentiles, perhaps put a stop to their kingdom work.

In about 49 AD the church in Antioch sent Barnabas and Paul with a team of believers, which included Titus (Gal 2:1), to discuss the issue with apostles and elders of the Council of Jerusalem led by the disciples Peter and James, the brother of Jesus.

Significantly, Barnabas and Paul do more than travel to Jerusalem. They seize every opportunity to spread the news about Jesus and to encourage their fellow Christians.

> . . . as they traveled through Phoenicia and Samaria, they told how the Gentiles had been converted. This news made all the believers very glad (Acts 15:3).

Barnabas and Paul are welcomed in Jerusalem by the Christians. They share their ministry experiences before the discussion takes place about whether or not "Gentiles must be circumcised and required to keep the law of Moses" (Acts 15:5), which is proposed by the believers who are members of the "party of the Pharisees," the more conservative group of Jewish believers.

A lengthy discussion occurs. Peter shares his thoughts and experiences working with the Gentiles, and then Barnabas and Paul address the crowd.

> The whole assembly became silent as they listened to Barnabas and Paul telling about the signs and wonders God had done among the Gentiles through them (Acts 15:12).

The fact that Barnabas' name is mentioned first in this text implies that he is the leader of the delegation from Antioch. This is no surprise, as he has been a kingdom worker longer than Paul. Empowered by the Holy Spirit, experienced working with new Christians from different cultures, he clearly advocates for and would have stressed the importance of Christian unity. He is a visionary who sees how the new covenant—the *new* relationship between God and people mediated by Jesus—extends to the Gentiles (the uncircumcised).

Barnabas and Paul's faith and commitment to church unity result in the Council of Jerusalem's decision that Gentile Christians do not have to observe the Mosaic Law. James states:

> It is my judgment, therefore, that we should not make it difficult for the Gentiles who are turning to God. Instead we should write to them, telling them to abstain from food polluted by idols, from sexual immorality, from the meat of strangled animals and from blood. For the law of Moses has been preached in every city from the earliest times and is read in the synagogues every Sabbath (Acts 15:19–21).

Paul also writes in Galatians 2:9 that the Council meeting decides that he and Barnabas should take the Good News to the Gentiles across the Roman world, while Peter, James and John—the leading members of the Christian community in Jerusalem—would concentrate on witnessing to the Jews.[1]

The Council sends two of their leaders, Judas (called Barsabbas) and Silas, to accompany Barnabas and Paul and return to Syrian Antioch with the letter relaying the Council's decision.

> The people read it [the letter] and were glad for its encouraging message. Judas and Silas, who themselves were prophets, said much to encourage and strengthen the believers (Acts 15:31–33).

Paul's letter to the Galatians probably sums up this important decision for the future of Christianity: "There is neither Jew nor Gentile, neither slave nor free, nor is there male and female for you are all one in Christ Jesus" (Gal 3:28).

We sense the servant leadership qualities of Barnabas whenever he is mentioned in the Bible, most especially during this critical time in early Christian church history. He appears to be

---

1. Taylor, *The Bible Journey.*

respected, courageous, open-minded, and obedient to the guidance of the Holy Spirit. As he shares the gospel with many diverse cultures, he probably expresses creative and innovative thinking. He empathizes with his listeners as he inspires them to follow Jesus.

Barnabas exemplifies how to live the "first and greatest commandment, 'Love the Lord your God with all your heart and with all your soul and with all your mind'" (Matt 22:37). Charles Finney[2], writing in 1868, describes this Christian love:

> If Christian love is the love of the image of Christ in his people, then it can be exercised only where that image really or apparently exists. A person must reflect the image of Christ, and show the Spirit of Christ before other Christians can love him [or her] with the love of complacency.

Barnabas remains in ministry in Antioch until approximately 52 AD. Paul suggests they return to the towns they had visited during the first missionary journey to encourage the believers (Acts 15:36–37).

The sticking point occurs when Barnabas wishes to take John Mark with them and Paul disagrees. John Mark had returned home during the first missionary journey, though no reasons are given for his decision. The tension between Paul and Barnabas leads to Paul heading off with Silas on his second missionary journey, while Barnabas takes John Mark with him to Cyprus (Acts 15:36–41).

No matter who we are and whose we are, we experience tensions in our relationships with those who are near and dear to us, and even with fellow believers. Barnabas was no exception. During these challenging days he might have reflected on the suffering Jesus experienced as he was abandoned by most of those near and dear to him in the final hours of his life. Caroline Fletcher[3] captures thoughts Barnabas might have experienced.

---

2. Finney, *Lectures on Revivals.*
3. Fletcher, *Encounter with God*, 82.

. . . the crucifixion speaks to our suffering too. Because we know Christ experienced physical, emotional and mental anguish, it reminds us that, whatever we are facing, Jesus really does understand. . . . if we turn to God in our troubles, he can use our sufferings to mature our faith and strengthen our character.

Barnabas once again champions the underdog, John Mark, "the cousin of Barnabas" (Col 4:10). He sees the potential of John Mark and spends time with him in Cyprus, mentoring and training him as they share the Lord's work.

Barnabas had revealed strength of character as he advocated for John Mark against his good friend Paul. Later Paul and John Mark are reconciled (Col 4:10–11; 2 Tim 4:11) and John Mark becomes a valued member of the early Christian church. He became an assistant to Peter and is thought to have travelled with him to Rome. Tradition states that John Mark's gospel contained Peter's inspired teaching and experiences of his time with Jesus.

From this point on, Barnabas no longer appears in Acts, and Luke focuses totally on Paul's ministry.

Barnabas is mentioned briefly in 1 Cor 9:6 as Paul argues that he and Barnabas should not charge a fee for speaking. Those who undertook spiritual work, Paul suggested, should receive material support from those with whom they work.

There is a reference to Barnabas and Paul working together in Jerusalem with Titus (Col 2:1,9) and in another incident when Paul opposes Peter for yielding to the pressure of a Jewish circumcision group and possibly placing his friendship with Peter ahead of doctrinal truth (Gal 2:11–21).

> When Cephas [Peter] came to Antioch, I [Paul] opposed him to his face, because he stood condemned. For before certain men came to James, he used to eat with the Gentiles. But when they arrived, he began to draw back and separate himself from the Gentiles because he was afraid of those who belonged to the circumcision group. The other Jews joined him in his hypocrisy, so that by their hypocrisy even Barnabas was led astray (Galatians 2:11–13).

Incidents like these reassure us that no follower of Jesus is perfect, and remind us how all believers can be distracted when they choose to take their eyes off Jesus.

Church tradition states that Barnabas, thought to be the founder of the Cypriot Church, preached in Alexandria and Rome before being stoned to death at Salamis (in Cyprus) in 61 AD. Robin Branch[4] writes:

> Barnabas' words, actions, and life combined human kindness and God's blessings; quite likely his nickname reflected what God was doing in him and through him. Since it was *given* to him by the apostles, it shows how he consistently related to others.

Learnings from Barnabas—reach out with the love of Jesus

Any person who experiences non-judgmental, unconditional love and care when they are struggling—no matter the reason—might ask questions which eventually lead to a decision to follow Jesus. We are God's obedient messengers going where he asks us to go, doing what he wants us to do—in the power of the Holy Spirit— and loving others, as best as we can. Nineteenth century Scottish Presbyterian missionary to Nigeria Mary Slessor stated: "Christ sent me to preach the gospel and he will look after the results."

- We prayerfully seize every opportunity to share the unconditional love and grace of Jesus.

- We stay true to our convictions in our relationships with others—prayerfully.

- We are sensitive and respectful of others, their opinions and ideas. We appreciate that it is okay to respectfully agree to disagree.

- We learn how our actions often have more of an impact than our words.

4. Branch, *Barnabas*, 301.

- We appreciate that fellowship with other Christians is important in our spiritual growth.

- True stories—our testimony, for example—are a powerful way to share God's work. Most people identify with true stories to which they can relate.

Becoming a rippler—in the footsteps of Barnabas

Sacrificial love carries a personal cost. Inspired and guided by the Holy Spirit, we become positive agents of change for Jesus, transformational leaders in a global community desperate to receive unconditional love and encouragement. The following are a few love offering ideas for consideration.

Love your neighbor. . .

- Become a committed "prayer warrior."

- Wear a crucifix or some other item of Christian jewelry—walk tall for Jesus.

- Be a mediator; stay calm if there is a heated argument (attempt to look at the situation through the prayerful eyes and heart of Jesus).

- Give someone a Bible if they do not have one.

- Sell a luxury item and donate the proceeds to charity.

- Instead of receiving birthday or Christmas gifts, ask that the money be donated to a charity—a gift of love.

- Send cards to those being persecuted for their faith, for example, through Open Doors International—you could encourage this as a small group project.

- Make cards for children with cancer or some other serious illness—donate a toy, or game, or book—as you reach out to them with compassion.

- Hide notes of encouragement in the lunch box of family members.

- Give a basket baby shower for a foster family in which you pack commonly needed items—a love offering.

- Cancel a debt.

Love the Lord your God. . .

Blessed are the peacemakers,
For they will be called children of Jesus (Matt 5:9).

As we feel empowered by the Holy Spirit, we become peacemakers who strive to live nonviolent lives. We acknowledge that we are not always right and are dependent on God's guiding hand. We possess a desire to share God's unconditional love and peace with others, and appreciate that walking the Christian road comes at a cost. Our spiritual journey moves to a deeper, more trusting level. We step out in faith and become more involved in our community— "For the Spirit God gave us does not make us timid, but gives us power, love and self-discipline" (2 Tim 1:7).

- Volunteer to help with a Special Olympics event.

- Sponsor a daily Bible readings booklet for someone for a year.

- Volunteer either to read to a person who is visually impaired, or to spend time chatting to them.

- Help out in the family or extended family—clean, support, teach, coach, listen to a family member—love until it hurts.

- Where appropriate, volunteer to serve as a crossing guard at a local school.

- Volunteer at a summer camp attended by disadvantaged children or children who have lost a parent, or at another youth camp run by a church or charitable group.

- Help out at a local woman's shelter, or at a refugee center or camp.

- Visit people in prison, or in hospitals.

- Volunteer to join a community mentoring program.

- Adopt a grandparent—someone on their own who would welcome your compassion and care.

- Adopt a child.

> The will of God will never take you to where the grace of God will not protect you. To gain that which is worth having, it may be necessary to lose everything else.
> —Bernadette Devlin

In your precious name I pray

Prayer is the greatest power God has put into our hands for
service—praying is harder than doing, at least I find it so,
but the dynamic lies that way to advance the kingdom.
—Mary Slessor

*Reflections: Bring to mind a time when you encouraged
someone. How did you feel at the time—and now as you reflect
on that experience? What part did prayer play during that
time—and today in your life? Think about some of the ways
you praise and honor the name of Jesus each day?*

The Barnabas' approach—summary

Today, despite persecution in some countries, the global church
continues to grow, yet this was not the case immediately after the
death of Jesus when many of his followers fled Jerusalem in fear of
their lives.

Then came the day of Pentecost and the challenge of Peter
to the gathering crowd of "God-fearing Jews from every nation
under heaven" (Acts 2:5).

> Repent and be baptized every one of you, in the name of
> Jesus Christ for the forgiveness of your sins. And you will
> receive the gift of the Holy Spirit. The promise is for you

and your children and for all who are far off—for whom the Lord our God will call (Acts 2:38–39).

About three thousand were converted and the movement of the kingdom workers to bring praise, honor, and glory to God throughout the Roman Empire and beyond was under way (Acts 2:42–47). Enter Barnabas' ministry.

Pause and reflect for a moment on the importance of what Barnabas possibly witnessed during these days of the early church. Author and spiritual leader Roberts Liardon[1] noted:

> While Peter had been a coward and denied Christ three times on the night before Jesus' crucifixion [Luke 22:33; Luke 22:54-62], on the day of Pentecost he stepped up before the crowd and proclaimed that Jesus was the Messiah, to such effect that three thousand were saved that day. In the words of many who have looked at this situation, "Something definitely happened to inspire that change," and this is one of the evidences given time and again for the resurrection of Jesus. Something tremendous happened to make that change, and it couldn't have been the disciples stealing away Jesus' body in the dead of night, because Peter never could have come up with such conviction if he had known it was all a fraud.

By the time of his death, Barnabas had modeled the meaning of selfless, sacrificial, Christlike service—despite his imperfections—and had played a decisive role in the formation of the early Christian church.

From the moment Barnabas made a commitment to follow Jesus, he moved out of his comfort zone and his life took on new meaning and purpose. The kingdom work, guided by the power of the Holy Spirit, would determine his future path. He modeled one of the key hallmarks of salvation when he rejected greed and the right to his financial control, sold land and generously donated the proceeds to spread the gospel (Acts 4:36–37).

In effect, this generous gesture from Barnabas became a model of a selfless Christian lifestyle: listen and respond to the

---

1. Liardon, *The Smith Wigglesworth Prophecy*, 92.

needs of others; share possessions; authentically care for one another and their needs; do everything with a joyful heart giving praise and honor to God; and be obedient to the guidance of the Holy Spirit. Author, pastor and theologian Dan Lioy[2] wrote: "While Barnabas lived in the present, his heart was planted in the soil of God's eternal kingdom."

God calls us to hold our possessions lightly. *Everything we have comes from him.* "It gives it to us as a trust to be managed— not a treasure to be hoarded."[3]

Barnabas reached out and championed others when fellow believers excluded them. The key examples are when Barnabas traveled to Tarsus to call Saul a number of years after the latter's conversion (Acts 9:26–27); and the way he defended John Mark, then mentored and trained him in Cyprus (Acts 15:36–41). Paul and Mark became significant members of the early Christian church movement which laid the foundations for the spread of the gospel into the global community. Author and pastor Jerry Ferrso[4] noted:

> It is a risk to reach out to people and love them, invest in them, care for them, and mentor them. However, if we fail in these areas the church's mission will be highly impacted in a negative way.

Barnabas later teamed up with Paul for the first missionary journey, stepping aside with humility during this journey to allow Paul to become the chief spokesman (Acts 11:25; 12:25–14:28). They obeyed Jesus' instruction: "Go into all the world and preach the gospel to all creation. Whoever believes and is baptized will be saved, but whoever does not believe will be condemned" (Mark 16:15–16).

Barnabas contributed significantly to the building of an "international" church and displayed exceptional servant leadership skills. Guided by the Holy Spirit, he modeled how to minister to

2. Lioy, *43 facts and lessons*, 9.

3. *Word in Life Bible*, 1681.

4. Ferrso, *Be a Barnabas*, 2.

diverse cross-cultural, multilingual communities. He was sincere and trusted by the early Christians (Acts 11:30) and, as Charles Finney[5] noted: "The apostles planted the Christian religion among the nations by the exercise of self-denial."

Barnabas exemplified how ordinary people, filled with the Holy Spirit, can apply their faith in Christlike service to their community and be a model for building positive social relationships. The Peace Prayer of Saint Francis is a helpful prayer to keep us focused on our ministry to honor, praise, and serve Jesus as we walk in the footsteps of Barnabas (Appendix 2). Leadership expert John Gordon[6] could have been describing Barnabas when he wrote:

> You serve others by investing in them: you develop them, encourage them, uplift them, inspire them . . . the more you serve the people below you, and the more you empower and encourage them, the more likely they are to perform at a higher level and actually raise you and your organization to another level.

Barnabas showed courage and perseverance and a steadfast trust in God during his ministry. He "walked the talk" and spoke God's truth no matter what the outcome might be. He was threatened, forced out of areas, returned to encourage believers to persevere and, according to church tradition, was put to death for his beliefs. He modeled servant leadership as expressed by leadership experts Ken Blanchard and Phil Hodges[7]:

> The fruit of great servant leadership is realized when a leader seeks to send the next generation of leaders to meet the challenges of their season with all the wisdom, knowledge and spiritual resources he or she can provide.

Barnabas and Paul carried out their work with the right motives and always from the heart. They planted churches wherever they traveled and then did their best to encourage, nurture, and mentor the elders in these churches. They modeled how a small

5. Finney, *Lectures on Revivals.*
6. Barna, *Master Leaders.*
7. Blanchard and Hodges, *Lead like Jesus.*

group of people could come together to praise and worship God, pray together, and open their hearts to the guidance of the Holy Spirit to do kingdom work, and then observe how their numbers multiplied—one of the strong themes in Acts: "They [the believers] devoted themselves to the apostles' teaching and to fellowship, to the breaking of bread and to prayer" (Acts 2:42).

Learning from Barnabas—a summary of Christlike qualities

We reflect on seven key qualities which Barnabas consistently modeled and which encourage us to expand our good intentions, impact many more lives, and place these efforts at the center of our eternal journey.

1. Service—Barnabas modeled selfless, sacrificial servant leadership—epitomized by Jesus' willingness to give up his life so others can be saved—placing the needs of others first and encouraging them to fulfill their God-given potential. He was teachable, self-controlled, patient, and open-minded— "Therefore, as God's chosen people, holy and dearly loved, clothe yourselves with compassion, kindness, humility, gentleness and patience" (Col 3:12). Author Melody Beattie wrote: "Live your life from your heart. Share your heart. And your story will touch and heal people's souls."

2. Authentic—at all times Barnabas appeared to be honest and trustworthy. He genuinely cared for others, and reached out to them with respect, empathy, and courage—"in everything set them an example by doing what is good. In your teaching show integrity, seriousness, and soundness of speech that cannot be condemned, so that those who oppose you may be ashamed because they have nothing bad to say about us" (Titus 2:7–8). He was a "people's person" unafraid to be himself at all times. In all likelihood he learnt when and how to be vulnerable, and appreciated the importance of a forgiving heart—"For if you forgive other people when they sin against you, your heavenly Father will also forgive you. But if you do

not forgive others their sins, your Father will not forgive your sins" (Matt 6:14–15).

3. Respect—Barnabas modeled respect towards all those with whom he interacted, a key quality when communicating with diverse communities. Everyone probably felt valued and heard: "So, we say with confidence, 'The Lord is my helper; I will not be afraid. What can mere mortals do to me?'" (Heb 13:16). He collaborated with others and appeared to look beyond self-interest. Bill Palmer[8] wrote:

> If we want to be more like Barnabas, we will also be faced with choices about how we view our brothers and sisters. If we want to be advocates, standing beside them, we must first believe in them. We must believe in their value before God, and we must choose to consider their future rather than dwell on sins and mistakes of the past.

4. Nurture—Barnabas, the encourager, moved alongside new believers in a non-judgmental, caring way, connected them with other believers and resources and played a key role in the building of the early church—"Carry each other's burdens, and in this way you will fulfill the law of Christ" (Gal 6:2). New believers probably felt safe and secure in the welcoming atmosphere he created, which allowed them to grow spiritually. He was an effective listener who inspired and motivated others such as Paul and John Mark to undertake significant kingdom work.

5. Inspire—Barnabas' gift of encouragement, combined with a generous heart and an optimistic and joyful attitude to praise and glorify Jesus, strengthened and motivated the early church movement. Joy is characteristic of a life of faith, a gift of the Holy Spirit (Gal 5:22), as well as an emotion. Barnabas became a valued signpost pointing people to Jesus. He was a messenger of hope, who believed God is always present, is

8. Palmer, *Learning from Barnabas*.

working out his plan, and has gone into the future ahead of us (Mark 12:28–30).

6. Accountable—Barnabas took his ministry seriously, evident by the way he fasted, prayed, sought guidance from the Holy Spirit, contributed to a team culture, remained humble, and was a positive person of significant influence who sought to be a man of peace—"Let the peace of Christ rule in your hearts, since as members of one body you were called to peace. And be thankful" (Col 3:15). Charles Finney[9] reminds us never to underestimate the power of prayer: "Prayer prepares the channels for the Holy Spirit to fill and flow through and out into the world."

7. Bless—through his selfless, sacrificial lifestyle Barnabas anointed many new believers. He nurtured, mentored, and encouraged them. He modeled the Beatitudes outlined by Jesus in the Sermon on the Mount, as we have seen through the pages of this book (Matt 5:3–10).

> One cannot obtain a Christlike character for nothing;
> one cannot do a Christlike work save at a great price.
> —James Hudson Taylor[10]

Becoming a rippler—in the footsteps of Barnabas

Selfless, sacrificial Christian living is a lifelong journey, so we must be patient and kind to ourselves as we travel on the eternal path.

Barnabas modeled the importance of daily fellowship with other believers. He also modeled how self-discipline becomes a key quality during this journey through the lifestyle he led. It is helpful to establish a time each day to read the Bible, meditate and reflect on its message, to converse with God *and* to listen to him. Pastor and author Henry Clay Fish stated: "The Bible is the battery through which the Holy Spirit illuminates and saves."

9. Finney, *Lectures on Revivals.*
10. Taylor, *Hudson Taylor's Spiritual Secret,* 27.

Love your neighbor...

Some helpful teachings from experienced Christian trailblazers can encourage and guide our thinking and planning. We can allow them to inspire us to continually seek God's guidance as we remember all who suffered in the Holocaust—especially the 1.5 million children—and in other major global events over the years, so we can become positive agents of change.

Fanny Crosby[11], the great composer of more than eight thousand gospel songs—"Blessed Assurance," "To God be the Glory," "Praise Him! Praise Him!"—was blind as a result of the carelessness of her doctor shortly after her birth. She wrote:

> It seemed intended by the blessed Providence of God that I should be blind all my life and I thank him for the dispensation. . . . I could not have written thousands of hymns if I had been hindered by the distractions of seeing all the interesting and beautiful objects that would have been presented to my notice.

James Hudson Taylor reflected on his preparations for his missionary work in China:

> . . . my experience was that the less I spent on myself [financially] and the more I gave to others, the fuller of happiness and blessings did my soul become.
> —James Hudson Taylor[12]

Evangelist William Young Fullerton[13], one of the assistants of the well-known Christian preacher and leader Charles Hadden Spurgeon, wrote of him:

> To me he is master and friend. I have neither known nor heard of any other, in my time, so many-sided, so commanding, so simple, so humble, so selfless, so entirely Christ's man.

11. Wiersbe, *50 people*, 102.
12. Taylor, *Hudson Taylor's Spiritual Secret*, 27.
13. Wiersbe, *50 People*, 142.

Southern Baptist missionary Lottie Moon[14], who spent nearly forty years with the Foreign Mission Board living and working in China, shared these thoughts in January 1889:

> Please say to the new missionaries that they are coming to a life of hardship, responsibility and constant self-denial. They must live, the greater part of the time in Chinese houses, in close contact with people. They will be alone in the interior and will need to be strong and courageous. If the joy of the Lord be their strength, the blessedness of the work will more than compensate for its hardships. Let them come "rejoicing to suffer" for the sake of the Lord and Master who freely gives his life for them.

Brother Lawrence[15] offered a word of encouragement as relevant today as it was when he wrote in the seventeenth century:

> Take courage! God often allows us to go through difficulties to purify our souls and to teach us to rely on him more (1 Peter 1:6–7). So, offer him your problems unceasingly, and ask him for the strength to overcome them. Talk to him often; forget him as seldom as possible. Praise him. When the difficulties are at their worst, go to him humbly and lovingly—as a child goes to a loving father—and ask for the help you need from his grace.

The great nineteenth century evangelist Frederick Brotherton Meyer[16] described what being a committed follower of Jesus meant:

> . . . a condition of mind in which one becomes blessedly oblivious to what men say or do, so long as the light of his approval shines warm and fresh upon the heart.

Evangelist Joseph Parker[17] said of Frederick Brotherton Meyer: "He never leaves me without the impression that I have been face to face with a man of God." Spurgeon said of Meyer: "Meyer preaches as a man who has seen God face to face."

14. International Mission Board.
15. Lawrence, *The practice*, 51.
16. Wiersbe, *50 People*, 214.
17. Wiersbe, *50 People*, 218.

Gladys Aylward, the British-born twentieth century evangelical missionary to China, provides a wonderful example of selfless service, despite her lack of education and humble beginnings:

> I wasn't God's first choice for what I've done in China . . . I don't know who it was . . . it must have been a man . . . a well-educated man. I don't know what happened. Perhaps he died. Perhaps he wasn't willing . . . and God looked down . . . and saw Gladys Aylward . . . and God said, "Well, she's willing."

A final word from Brother Lawrence[18]:

> I still believe that all spiritual life consists of preaching God's presence, and that anyone who practices it correctly will soon attain spiritual fulfillment. To accomplish this, it is necessary for the heart to be emptied of everything that would offend God. He wants to possess your heart completely. Before any work can be done in your soul, God must be totally in control. There is no sweeter manner of living in the world than continuous communion with God.

Love the Lord your God. . .

Blessed are those who are persecuted
because of righteousness,
for theirs is the kingdom of heaven (Matt 5:10).

Jesus modeled the cost of selflessly serving God. He spoke many times about the persecution of those who follow him—"Blessed are you when people insult you, persecute you and falsely say all kinds of evil against you because of me. Rejoice and be glad, because great is your reward in heaven for in the same way they persecuted the prophets who were before you" (Matt 5:11–12).

As we draw closer to Jesus and are empowered by the Holy Spirit to respond to God's call on our life, we understand how we

18. Lawrence, *The practice*, 29.

are *in* this world, yet *not of it.* "Do not conform to the pattern of this world, but be transformed by the renewing of your mind. Then you will be able to test and approve what God's will is—his good, pleasing and perfect will" (Rom 12:2). We are no longer self-sufficient. We depend on God alone. While we might be persecuted when we stand tall for Jesus—or identify with Jesus—we persevere with courage and the assurance that we will be blessed eternally in the kingdom of heaven:

> We are hard pressed on every side, but not crushed; perplexed, but not in despair; persecuted, but not abandoned; struck down, but not destroyed. We always carry around in our body the death of Jesus, so that the life of Jesus may also be revealed in our body. For we who are alive are always being given over to death for Jesus' sake, so that his life may also be revealed in our mortal body (2 Cor 4:8–11).

Jesus tell us, through the Beatitudes, to "Go and do . . ." and there is always a cost. How are we following Jesus today? This is a good question for us to ask as we grow in our eternal faith walk, individually, and collaboratively.

Barnabas witnessed the impact of the death and resurrection of Jesus on communities. He chose to follow Jesus no matter the cost. Barnabas was assertive because he knew who he was and *whose* he was.

The Barnabas Prayer is my response to the question: *Whose am I?*

What choice will you make? As you reflect on this question, gain encouragement and inspiration from the words of author and evangelist Dr. Michael Cassidy[19]: "Aim to finish better than you started, remembering too that when this Day is done the best is yet to be, because Heaven is our Final Home."

> Do all the good you can, by all the means you can, in all the ways you can, in all the places you can, at all the times you can, to all the people you can, as long as you ever can.
> —John Wesley

19. Cassidy, *Footprints*, 446.

Appendix 1

Dropping Pebbles in the Stream[1]

Drop a pebble in the water: just a splash, and it is gone;
But there's half-a-hundred ripples circling on and on and on,
Spreading, spreading from the center, flowing on out to the sea;
And there is no way of telling where the end is going to be.

Drop a pebble in the water: in a minute you forget;
But there's little waves a-flowing, and there's ripples circling yet,
And those little waves a-flowing to a great big wave have grown;
You've disturbed a mighty river just by dropping in a stone.

Drop an unkind word, or careless: in a minute it is gone;
But there's half-a-hundred ripples circling on and on and on.
They keep spreading, spreading, spreading from the center as they go,
And there is no way to stop them, once you've started them to flow.

Drop an unkind word, or careless: in a minute you forget;
But there's little waves a-flowing, and there's ripples circling yet,
And perhaps in some sad heart a mighty wave of tears you've stirred,
And disturbed a life was happy ere you dropped that unkind word.

1. Foley, *Dropping Pebbles*, 17–18.

Drop a word of cheer and kindness: just a flash and it is gone;
But there's half-a-hundred ripples circling on and on and on,
Bearing hope and joy and comfort on each splashing, dashing wave
Till you wouldn't believe the volume of the one kind word you gave.

Drop a word of cheer and kindness: in a minute you forget;
But there's gladness still a-swelling, and there's joy a-circling yet,
And you've rolled a wave of comfort whose sweet music can be heard
Over miles and miles of water just by dropping one kind word.

—JAMES W. FOLEY (1874–1939), journalist, author, and a poet laureate
of North Dakota

Appendix 2

Peace Prayer of Saint Francis

Lord, make me an instrument of your peace:
where there is hatred, let me sow love;
where there is injury, pardon;
where there is doubt, faith;
where there is despair, hope;
where there is darkness, light;
where there is sadness, joy.

O divine master, grant that I may not so much seek
to be consoled as to console,
to be understood as to understand,
to be loved as to love.
For it is in giving that we are pardoned,
and it is in dying that we are born to eternal life.
Amen.

Acknowledgments

Thanks to many people over the years who have positively influenced my developing faith walk. There are too many to mention and they come from all walks of life.

When I felt God nudging me to write this book, I sent a very rough draft to some good friends and family members and requested their honest feedback. This feedback helped shape the content and style of the final book. Sincere thanks to Rudi Pakendorf, Mark Leam, David Cook, John Cox, and Jonathan Gale.

Special thanks, too, to my daughter, Trish, and my wife, Jane. They read a couple of drafts of the book at crucial times. My millennial daughter kept encouraging me: "Make it more conversational, dad. Soften the tone." Jane encouraged me to include the specific words from more Bible verses. I hope I managed to find the right tone and balance of content. Trish kindly used her creative talents to design the map, which appears at the beginning of the book, to show the areas where Barnabas helped set up the early church.

The Bibliography does not do justice to the resources I have used while writing this book. There is an extensive list of resources on my website www.yess.co.nz to give readers additional references for the content. If I have inadvertently failed to acknowledge a source, I would be most grateful if the reader would inform me of this so that I can rectify the omission before any further printings of this book.

ACKNOWLEDGMENTS

Sincere thanks to Matthew Wimer and the editors of Resource Publications of Wipf and Stock for all their support, help and guidance, without which this particular writing experience would not have been possible. Thank you for your faith in me.

To God be all glory and praise!

Bibliography

Adams, Jennifer, ed. *Harriet Newell, Delighting in Her Heavenly Bridegroom: The Memoirs of Harriet Newell, Teenage Missionary Wife.* Forest, VA: Corner Pillar, 2011.

Barna, George. *Master Leaders.* Carol Stream, IL: Barna, 2009.

Blanchard, Ken, and Phil Hodges. *Lead like Jesus—Lessons for Everyone from the Greatest Leadership Role Model of All Time.* Nashville: Thomas Nelson, 2005.

Brother Lawrence. *The Practice of the Presence of God.* Springdale, PA: Whitaker House, 1982.

Branch, Robin Gallaher. "Barnabas: Early Church Leader and Model of Encouragement." *Indie Skriflig* 41.2 (2007) 295–322.

Cassidy, Michael. *Footprints in the African Sand: My Life & Times.* London: SPCK, 2019.

Cox, Robin. *7 Key Qualities of Effective Teachers: Encouragement for Christian Educators.* Eugene, OR: Resource, 2020.

Coyle, Graham. *To Infinity and Turn Left: Exploring God's Purpose for Christian Teachers.* Independent, 2020. Kindle ed.

Fenelon. *Let Go: To Get Peace and Real Joy.* Banner: Springdale, PA: Whitaker, 1973.

Ferrso, Jerry. "Be a Barnabas: Three Lessons from the Life of Barnabas." https://ministry127.com/outreach-and-discipleship/be-a-barnabas.

Finney, Charles. "Lectures on Revivals of Religion." In *7 Classics on Revival: The Great Awakening, the Welsh Revival, Azusa Street, and More.* Grosse Pointe Park, MI: Dream, 2014. Kindle ed.

Fletcher, Caroline. *Encounter with God: Renew Your Mind, Engage Your World.* Milton Keynes, UK: Scripture Union New Zealand, 2020.

Foley, James W. *The Verses of James W. Foley.* Vol. 2, *Book of Plains and Prairie.* Bismarck, ND: Hoskins, 1907.

International Mission Board. www.imb.org.

Liardon, Roberts. *The Smith Wigglesworth Prophecy & the Greatest Revival of All Time.* New Kensington, PA: Whitaker House, 2013.

Lioy, Dan. "Barnabas: 43 Facts and Lessons from the Life of a Disciple." *Disciplr* (blog), n.d. https://disciplr.com/barnabas-facts-lessons.

Palmer, Bill. "Learning from Barnabas, the Son of Encouragement." *Discern Magazine*, March/April 2018.

Penn-Lewis, Jessie. *The Awakening in Wales and Some of the Hidden Springs.* New York: Revell, 1905.

Stead, William Thomas, and George Campbell Morgan. *The Welsh Revival (1905): Narrative of Facts, Source of Power.* Boston: Pilgrim, 1905.

Taylor, Chris, and Jenifer Taylor. *The Bible Journey.* www.thebiblejourney.org.

Taylor, Howard, and Geraldine Taylor. *Hudson Taylor's Spiritual Secret.* Chicago: Moody, 2009.

Volavkova, Hana, ed. *I Never Saw Another Butterfly: Children's Drawings and Poems from Terezin Concentration Camp 1942–1944.* New York: Schocken, 1993.

Word in Life Bible: Contemporary English Version. Nashville: Thomas Nelson, 1998.

Wiersbe, Warren W. *50 People Every Christian Should Know: Learning from Spiritual Giants of the Faith.* Grand Rapids, MI: Baker, 2009.

Printed in Australia
AUHW021255180221
341421AU00006B/6

9 781725 289611